Sylvia's SUPER-Awesome PROJECT Book

Volume 2

Super Simple Arduino!
by "Super-Awesome" Sylvia

SUPERAWESOMEBOOK.COM

Sylvia's Super-Awesome Project Book (Volume 2): Super-Simple Arduino, by "Super-Awesome" Sylvia Todd
© 2014 Constructing Modern Knowledge Press

Constructing Modern Knowledge Press **cmkpress.com**

ISBN: 978-0-9891511-6-0
JNF051090   JUVENILE NONFICTION / Technology / Electricity & Electronics

Series Editor: Gary S. Stager, Ph.D.
Art Direction: Lily Ross

Concept, design, and text by "Super-Awesome" Sylvia and James Todd.
Illustrations by Sylvia Todd.
Photos by Christian Koszka (**FreeTimePro.com**), and James Todd.
"Pigeons in Flight" (HEE-NC-65002) © 2010 MIT. Courtesy of MIT Museum.

Watch the companion video for this book, read blogs, post comments, or even submit your own show ideas on our website at **sylviashow.com.**

Special thanks to Gary Stager and Sylvia Martinez for their support and for helping to realize this project. Who knew squashed dead trees could be so fun to work with!

Also a huge thanks to my Dad, Mom, and the rest of my family for being there for me when I was pulling my hair out.

SylviaShow.com/Arduino

CONTENTS

THE BASICS 1
   Your Robot Friends! 1
   What's an Arduino?? 2
   Getting to Know Your Arduino 3
   The IDE and You 4
   Helpful Tips for Loading the Software 4
   Test Your Connection 5

PROJECT ONE: Simple Strobe 6

PROJECT TWO: R.I.F.F. 20

PROJECT THREE: The Tapper 30

MAKE MORE! (Resources) 38

PAINTBOT'S DOODLE CORNER 39

You can purchase a kit with *all* the parts you need for the three projects in this book at SparkFun.com/sylviakit

sparkfun ELECTRONICS

Hi! My name is Sylvia, I'm the maker of Sylvia's Super-Awesome Maker Show, a YouTube show I started when I was eight to encourage tinkerers of all ages to go out there and make something. I'm a kid just like you with three younger siblings. I love to draw, make, read, and write.

My tinkering and inventing have taken me to The White House (twice!), London, Rome and even the United Nations in Geneva! I love workshops and speaking at Maker Faires and schools all over the place.

This book introduces you to three super-simple projects my dad and I came up with to get your brain going. Whether you're a beginner looking for a first project, or an advanced electrical engineer, you will need almost nothing more than your computer and an Arduino board, so there's no reason not to try. (There's even extra stuff after each project to inspire you to do even more!)

The first two projects in this book are featured in my Super-Simple Arduino episode, which you can watch on my website at sylviashow.com/arduino. While you are there, you can also check out all my other awesome episodes.

Don't just sit there reading, let's go make something!

Sylvia

THE BASICS

Your Robot Friends!

Throughout this book series, you'll meet all sorts of friendly robots who are here to help you out! Let's meet a few of them:

SmartBot
Is just that. He's a clever robot who knows what's up. He shows us how things work, or gives a warning when something can be dangerous. Listen to SmartBot, and you'll be smart too!

ScienceBot
Testing ideas and hypotheses are what he was made for. Wherever you find ScienceBot, you're sure to find awesome, testable science facts or experiment ideas that you can try.

BuilderBot
Was built to build. She has a passion for using tools like her hammer, screwdriver, and soldering iron to take things apart and make new things. You'll find her wherever there's stuff to build, or a list of tools you're going to need.

CoderBot
Enjoys math, logic, programming, and making things work. You'll find her wherever coding or math stuff needs a good explanation.

PaintBot
Loves to create with a paintbrush, design with pencil, pen, and computer, craft with paper or cloth, and make things beautiful. You'll find PaintBot when it's time to get artistic and be creative!

DoodleBots
If the book is getting too boring, find the DoodleBots! They were made to hang around and have fun. Before long, you'll find something fun too.

Keep an eye out as you go through the book and look for other robot friends to help you on your way!

What's an Arduino??

The Arduino is an awesome programmable prototyping platform. It's a little computer that acts like a brain for robots, sensors, or other machines that connect to the real world. It's pretty inexpensive, too! For less than the cost of a tank of gas, you can get yourself this little blue open-source brain board and start creating something incredible. With just a little bit of code (that you don't even have to write), it can do almost any crazy thing you want.

RedBoard   Esplora   Due

Not to mention, Arduino boards now come in all shapes and sizes (some of them are shown above) with tons more processing power, and a variety of inputs and outputs. Only the blue Arduino boards are officially called "Arduino", offshoot boards like the RedBoard above are called Arduino-compatible. They can do everything an official blue Arduino can do, but look different and are made by someone else. For our experiments, we recommend the Arduino Uno or the Redboard, which are easy to get and simple to use.

When you get an Arduino, it's not always clear what you should do. I've heard of some people who get one, and then just leave it on the shelf — what a waste! With just a quick search online, you can find literally thousands of incredibly creative Arduino-based projects, like walking robots, musical instruments, or even video games. Thanks to the awesome Arduino community, most projects can be built at home with the parts listed and open-source code you simply copy-and-paste. Once your invention is working, you can change the code, add functionality, and make the machine your own.

Getting to Know Your Arduino

An Arduino can look a *little* scary, but don't worry, it's your **friend**. All the inputs and outputs use friendly standard jumper sockets connected to the big microcontroller chip in the middle, so you can plug things straight in and see results immediately. It also plugs into USB on almost any computer, so setup should be a snap! If you need help, search the internet for helpful tips, or check out the official Arduino website at **arduino.cc** for language reference, project ideas, and support.

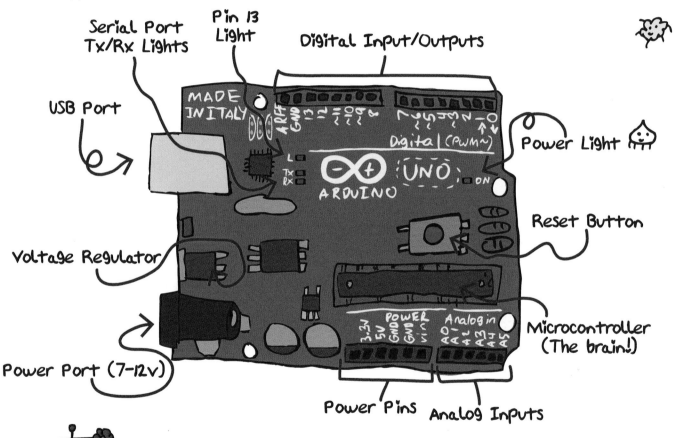

Serial Port Tx/Rx Lights

Pin 13 Light

Digital Input/Outputs

USB Port

Power Light

Voltage Regulator

Reset Button

Power Port (7-12v)

Microcontroller (The brain!)

Power Pins   Analog Inputs

Whether you want to make your own custom talking toy, or maybe a security system for your room, the Arduino system and community of super smart and helpful people have everything you need to help make your electronic dream a reality.

The IDE and You

The I.D.E. (**I**ntegrated **D**evelopment **E**nvironment), is a fancy name for a text editor. It's software on your computer that lets you write code as regular text, and then sends it – uploads it – to your Arduino. The IDE includes some fun, helpful extras like the compiler, upload button, and serial console. Your Arduino only holds one program, called a sketch, at a time. So, each time you upload a sketch, the Arduino forgets the old sketch and runs the new one.

Before you start to build the projects in this book, you should download and install the latest IDE software from the Arduino website, **www.arduino.cc**.

Helpful Tips for Setting Up Your IDE

If you are using Windows, make sure the Arduino driver installation is successful before continuing.

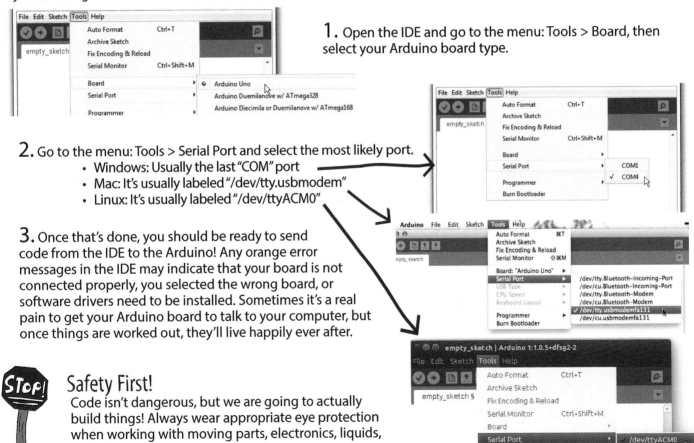

1. Open the IDE and go to the menu: Tools > Board, then select your Arduino board type.

2. Go to the menu: Tools > Serial Port and select the most likely port.
- Windows: Usually the last "COM" port
- Mac: It's usually labeled "/dev/tty.usbmodem"
- Linux: It's usually labeled "/dev/ttyACM0"

3. Once that's done, you should be ready to send code from the IDE to the Arduino! Any orange error messages in the IDE may indicate that your board is not connected properly, you selected the wrong board, or software drivers need to be installed. Sometimes it's a real pain to get your Arduino board to talk to your computer, but once things are worked out, they'll live happily ever after.

Safety First!

Code isn't dangerous, but we are going to actually build things! Always wear appropriate eye protection when working with moving parts, electronics, liquids, and chemicals!

Test Your Connection

 1. We need to know if the IDE is really talking to our Arduino board. To find out, we will load an example sketch that blinks the onboard pin 13 light. Go to menu and select File > Examples >Basics > Blink.

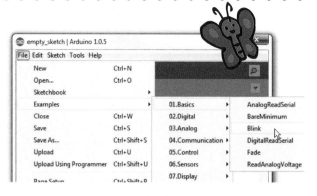

 2. When you see the sketch in the Arduino IDE, click Compile/Verify button and the compiler will check your If you see orange error messages, it's debugging time!

 3. Make sure your Arduino is plugged into your computer with a USB cable. Click the Upload button. If the compiler says everything is good, and your computer is talking to your Arduino, you should see your pin 13 light start flashing! Now we can have some fun!

> When you are uploading, the RX and TX lights should blink away on the Arduino, and in a few seconds, your code should be up and running! If not, check the helpful troubleshooting tips online at **www.arduino.cc/troubleshooting.**

 4. Now see if you can find something to change in the code that makes the pin 13 light blink faster or slower. Don't forget to upload the code after every change!

 ## Debugging 101

If you see an orange warning at the bottom of the IDE after you've verified your sketch, it means something is wrong and you'll need to fix it. Usually you missed a semicolon at the end of sentence, or made a silly typo. CompilerBot will try his best to tell you what he wants to see. If CompilerBot is happy and your code is uploaded, but it's *still* not working, you're going to need to try changing some variables, or check your wiring. We'll tell you more about CompilerBot later on. Just remember: Don't give up, find those bugs!

SIMPLE STROBE

For our first project, we'll be making a precisely controllable strobe! A strobe (or *stroboscope*), is a flashing light that you can use to slow down, reverse, or stop time for really fast moving things! Sort of. By flashing a light really quickly, stuff that happens too fast to see looks like it slows down or stops. This really cool illusion is pretty useful too. Ready to make one? ***Let's go!***

Parts Needed

- **An Arduino.** We like RedBoard and Uno.

- **USB cable to upload to the Arduino.**

- **One bright LED.** I chose blue 'cause it's bright and cool, but you can use any kind you want.

- **A potentiometer.** These have three leads or wires, and a rotating turny bit on top. You may have to twist some wires on the ends!

- **A computer.**

Have the Arduino software installed and ready. If you haven't done this yet, see page 4.

WHERE TO FIND PARTS

You can get Arduinos, jumper wires, LEDs, potentiometers and more at your local electronic component store, or online at great places like **SparkFun.com**, **Adafruit.com**, and **MakerShed.com**.

You can buy a kit with all the parts for all the projects in this book at **SparkFun.com/sylviakit**

Recycling:
Look for potentiometers in old radios or control dials. LEDs can be found almost anywhere these days, from keychain lights to blinky shoes!

Safety First!

If you or someone you're working with suffers from photosensitive epilepsy, this isn't the project for you! Flashing lights can trigger seizures, and that's no fun. We recommend skipping to the next fun project (though there's nothing stopping you from reading about the project and checking out SmartBot's Thinking Lab).

Let's Build!

1. Push your LED's legs into the Arduino.

Push the *longer* leg of the LED into **pin 13**, and the *shorter* leg into **"GND"** (ground). Another name for the LED's legs are "leads."

What's my LED doing in the ground?

When electricity flows through wires in a circuit, it can do things like turn on lights or motors, react to switches, get information from sensors or dials, etc. Every electronic circuit needs a "ground" to complete it. Without a connection between a positive voltage and ground, the electricity won't flow anywhere!

If your electricity doesn't move, it can't do any work. Think of the electricity in a battery like water in a bottle. With the cap on the bottle, it won't move, but with the cap off and a clear path, water will flow happily to the ground. While that water flows, you can cause it to move a water wheel... or make your shoes wet.

What's so special about pin 13?

Pin 13 on the Arduino is pretty special and perfect for powering LEDs. If you look closely, you can see an itty-bitty LED on the board (pin 13 light on page 3 diagram) above the two LEDs labeled TX and RX. Usually marked with an "L", this LED is hooked up to pin 13 through a resistor, so without anything other than your Arduino, you can make it blink! If we let our LED be powered by the full 5 volts from another pin without a resistor, we'll fry it! Always use an appropriate resistor if lighting an LED from any Arduino pin other than 13.

2. Plug in the potentiometer.

First connect the outer leads into the 5v pin and a GND pin. Then, push the middle lead into one of the analog pins. I chose pin 2, 'cause it's the coolest of the analog pins! This allows you to very carefully send voltage between 0 and 5v to the analog pin.

What's this turn-y thing??

It's a potentiometer! They can be a knob or slider, and they change how much current moves through them as you slide or turn it! They can dim lights, control volume, or even act as direct input into an Arduino! Try to find potentiometers in stuff you use every day.

3. Input the code below into your IDE, verify it, and upload to the Arduino.

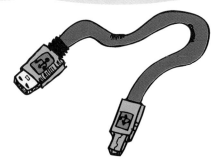

Complete and updated code can be found at **superawesomebook.com/strobe**, but why not test your typing skills and enter this into the Arduino IDE yourself? Copying and pasting is for *wimps!*

When the Arduino is connected to your computer, it gets power from the computer. Once you upload a program to the Arduino, you can unplug the USB cable, but your invention will need power either from an A/C adapter or a special battery connected directly to the Arduino board.

SimpleStrobe

```
// Gray text with two slashes are just helpful comments, you don't need to type them.  :)

int analogPin = 2; // Where our potentiometer will get plugged in.
int ledPin = 13; // Where our LED will get plugged in.
int onTime = 250; // Microseconds (millionths of a second) the LED will stay ON for a flash.

int minDelay = 1; // Minimum delay between strobe flashes in milliseconds (thousandths of a second).
int maxDelay = 100; // Maximum delay between strobe flashes (in milliseconds).
int strobeDelay = 0; // Placeholder variable where we'll store the actual delay.

void setup() {
  pinMode(ledPin, OUTPUT); // Setup ledPin as an output.
}

void loop() {
  // To make the math easier, we use map(value, fromMin, fromMax, toMin, toMax) to convert the
  // 0 to 1023 range we get from analogRead, into our strobe delay range of 1 to 100 :D
  strobeDelay = map(analogRead(analogPin), 0, 1023, minDelay, maxDelay);

  digitalWrite(ledPin, HIGH); // Switch the ledPin to HIGH, turn it on!
  delayMicroseconds(onTime); // Delay while on, for the given onTime.
  digitalWrite(ledPin, LOW); // Switch the ledPin to LOW, turn if off!
  delay(strobeDelay); // Delay while off, for given strobeDelay.
}
```

More About Code & the IDE

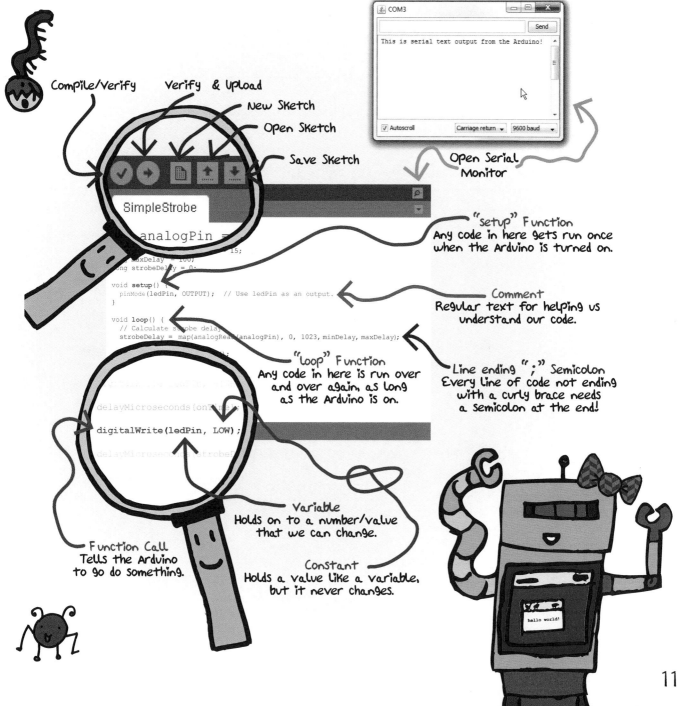

Compile/Verify

Verify & Upload

New Sketch

Open Sketch

Save Sketch

Open Serial Monitor

COM3

Send

This is serial text output from the Arduino!

Autoscroll   Carriage return   9600 baud

SimpleStrobe

```
analogPin =
           15;
maxDelay = 100;
ong strobeDelay = 0;

void setup() {
  pinMode(ledPin, OUTPUT);  // Use ledPin as an output.
}

void loop() {
  // Calculate strobe delay
  strobeDelay = map(analogRead(analogPin), 0, 1023, minDelay, maxDelay);



  delayMicroseconds(on

  digitalWrite(ledPin, LOW);

  delayMicroseconds strobe
```

"setup" Function
Any code in here gets run once when the Arduino is turned on.

Comment
Regular text for helping us understand our code.

"loop" Function
Any code in here is run over and over again, as long as the Arduino is on.

Line ending " ; " Semicolon
Every line of code not ending with a curly brace needs a semicolon at the end!

Function Call
Tells the Arduino to go do something.

Variable
Holds on to a number/value that we can change.

Constant
Holds a value like a variable, but it never changes.

11

EXPERIMENT TIME: ADJUSTABLE STROBE

Get an adult to help remove the front grill of a desk fan so we can see it better. If they don't trust you with an open fan, get one of those battery-operated ones with the foam squishy blades. That will do the trick!

Now just turn on the Arduino, and turn off the lights! Adjust the potentiometer until you lock into the phase/speed of the fan. If you've made your strobe without a potentiometer, just replace the code "analogRead(analogPin)" with some number between 0 and 1023. Try different values and re-upload your code. Lower numbers are faster, higher numbers are slower. Every fan moves at a different speed, so this will take some tweaking!

How it works:

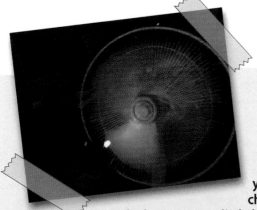

What is a Strobe?

Strobes (or *stroboscobes*) are really just lights that flash on really quickly, then turn off for an exact amount of time. By turning your potentiometer (or if you don't have one, changing your input number by hand), you change the time between flashes to be a little more, or a little less. Strobes can actually help you see things that move really fast. When your eyes see only black between one flash and another, the last image "freezes" in your mind and sticks together with the next one. As this happens again and again, it can make things look slow or stopped.

If you can, put numbers on each fan blade and see if you can read them with the strobe while it's spinning. Two common ways your strobe can sync up with the fan blades: one flash for every blade (every number will flip in sequence as it moves into the position of the last), or a single flash for every full revolution — a perfect match! There's an infinite number of crazy ways for it to sync, as every multiple of the number of fan blades to the strobe flashes per rotation will appear to sync up.

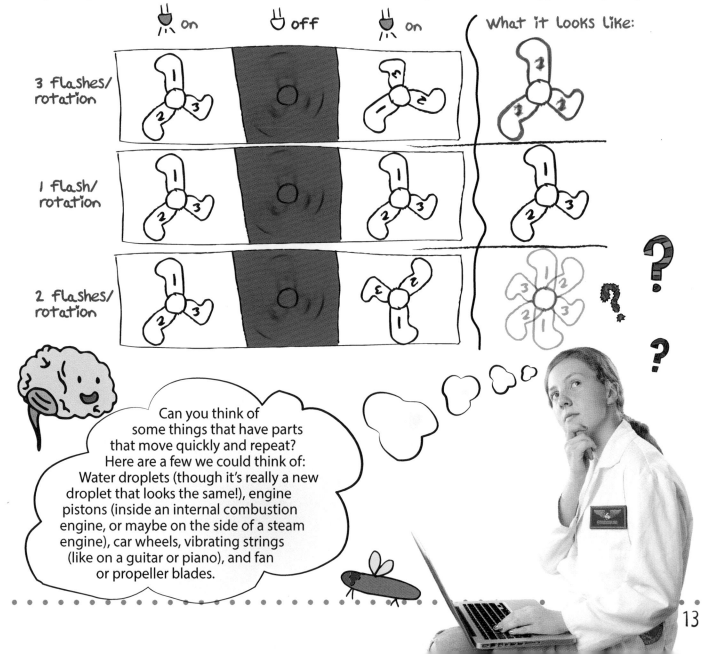

Can you think of some things that have parts that move quickly and repeat? Here are a few we could think of: Water droplets (though it's really a new droplet that looks the same!), engine pistons (inside an internal combustion engine, or maybe on the side of a steam engine), car wheels, vibrating strings (like on a guitar or piano), and fan or propeller blades.

Understanding Code

When you want to tell a computer what to do, you quickly learn that it doesn't speak your language. That's why a bunch of smart peeps came up with **programming languages** that computers can understand. Arduino uses a pretty old but very good language called "**C**". Every Arduino program is a list of instructions written in the C language that tells the Arduino to do something exactly same way, every time the program runs. It's mostly English, with a bit of *syntax* to make it more standard. It can be a little hard to read at first, but just pick out stuff you know, and the rest will start making sense.

The Arduino may be small, but it's very fast. It can do things faster than a millionth of a second, and we're going to use that to our advantage for this project. Once your simple strobe is assembled, you need to teach it to work by programming it. We do so by writing a program (or changing someone else's program). Today, lots of people call their computer programs, "code," and the programming process, "coding."

Key Words

SYNTAX: Word glue! Special words like `if`, `else`, `void`; mathematical stuff like +, −, *, =, %; and logic like `!` (not), `&&` (and).

SKETCH: The text or code of a software program written for the Arduino. We use the IDE to write, save, and load sketches.

FUNCTION: Computer instructions that perform some action or respond to triggers like buttons or sensors.

SETUP: The first function you'll see in most Arduino sketches. This code is run first before anything else, and it's only run once when the Arduino powers up.

LOOP: This is the second and most important function! Required for every sketch, it's where the Arduino does all the work, looping over and over again on the same code to do whatever you want!

VARIABLE: A special word that represents a letter or number that can change. We show variables as **green** in this book, though they're black in the IDE.

Every Arduino *sketch* has at least two *functions*: `setup` and `loop`. The `setup` function is triggered ONLY when the Arduino starts up. Then, the `loop` function runs and when it's done, it runs again, forever! Using just these two functions, you can make the Arduino do almost anything you want.

The Compiler

The "compiler" is part of the IDE that takes all the human readable code you write, and turns it into something that the little computer on the Arduino can understand. CompilerBot is our friend, but he is strict about the rules of code and syntax. When you think you are done, he will come in and tell you, "*You forgot a semicolon!*" or "*You can't give that dog an integer!*" He may complain to you, but getting to understand what he's trying to tell you is one of the **best** things you can learn. If your code is compiled and uploaded, we can start to experiment!

14

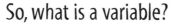

So, what is a variable?

Variables in code work just like they do in algebra. If you haven't worked with algebra yet, you can think of them like… a dog! Let's take a value that we want to keep track of (like a number or a word), write it on a piece of paper, and give that to our pooch. In this example, we call our variable dog "`onTime`". Now anytime we write "`onTime`" in our code, our doggy will give us back the last value we gave him on his paper.

VARIABLE DATA TYPES

`bit`: 0 or 1, that's it for the bit!

`bool`: Short for "boolean", either **`true`** or **`false`**: Kinda like the bit, but with words.

`byte`: 8 bits! Really it's just a number up to 255.

`char`: Holds a single letter from the keyboard, like **`'A'`**.

`int`: Short for "integer". Holds whole numbers from -32,768 to 32,767.

`long`: Can hold really, really big positive and negative numbers! Like millions and millions.

Defining a variable

Arduino C is a "strongly typed" language, which means you need to say what *kind* of value your variable will hold on to. So if we say he's an "`int`" dog, then he will be able to hold onto whole numbers. This is called the **data type**. When making your variables, just put the type right before the name.

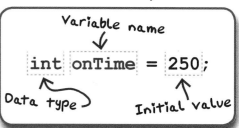

Using variables

To use a variable in your code, simply write the name of your variable in place of the value wherever you want to use it. In our example, we use the variable "`onTime`" to hold the number of microseconds (millionths of a second) the LED will stay on during a flash. Not only does it hold the first value you give it, a variable can also change value as your program runs, like giving your dog a new number to hold onto! In this project, we use the variable, "`strobeDelay`" that gets set in each loop as you adjust your potentiometer.

```
int spot = 1; // Variable "spot" now equals 1
int rover = spot + 1; // "rover" now equals 2

// Output "3" to the serial port
Serial.print(rover + spot);
```

It doesn't matter what you name your variables, as long as you're consistent, and the name helps you understand what it does. You can use single letters as names, like "**`x`**", but that isn't very helpful. Long names make more sense, but take longer to type.

Write it right!

Spaces aren't allowed in file, variable, or function names, so there are two popular ways of naming them using short phrases.

camelCase: first letter is lower, butEveryWordAfterStartsWithUppercase

all_lower: use_an_underscore_with_no_capital_letters

15

All About LEDs!

A diode is a thing that will only let electricity flow through them in ONE direction. LEDs (or light emitting diodes) are really just diodes that emit light. When the electricity flows the right direction in an LED, you get light!

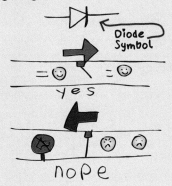

You can tell the polarity of an LED in two easy ways:

The long leg is called the anode (or positive lead).

The short leg is called the cathode (or negative lead). This hooks up to Ground in our strobe. Just think: short = gnd = smaller.

If your LED's legs have been cut off, they built in a cool little safety feature: the side of the body without a ridge on the bottom should be the same side as the negative lead.

Let's Play!

ScienceBot's Experiment Ideas

All science starts with a question! Here are a few to get your brain going.

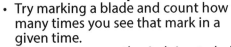

How fast does a fan spin?

- Try marking a blade and count how many times you see that mark in a given time.
- Can you program the Arduino to help you calculate this?

Can you use your strobe to measure how far something travels, or its average speed?

- If you use the value from before, you might be able to use the circumference to help.

What is the fastest you can blink a light once and still see it turn on? Does this speed change in daylight or in a dark room?

BuilderBot's Challenges

These are some cool ideas to make your project look a little cooler, do more, or just get more organized.

Try mounting your strobe in a mint tin with a battery and an on/off switch.

- Be sure to insulate the bottom with paper/plastic sticky tape! If you don't, all the pins could touch the metal container, and it would just be like connecting all of them together, which might mean a **DEAD ARDUINO! :(**

Add an LCD screen to display interesting stuff like the `strobeDelay` or estimated RPMs (Revolutions Per Minute)!

Add magnets to your strobe and stick it somewhere to make it more mobile or stable.

CoderBot's Challenges

These are "advanced" challenges for coders who aren't afraid to look stuff up, try new things, be curious, and go nuts!

There are a lot of sample sketches provided by the Arduino community that you can change or customize for your own projects. They're found by going into the File menu in the IDE and browsing the examples by category.

Make the strobe work with a button instead of a potentiometer.
- *See:* Examples > Digital > Button
- Use a variable to hold on to the delay number, wait for a button press, change the number when the button is down. Easy, right? ;)

Change the code to have the LED blink letters and words using Morse code.
- Morse code is just a series of dots and dashes with some space in between. The `delay()` function is your friend!
- You'll have to write a lot less code if you learn to make your own functions to do repetitive work for you. Skip ahead to page 34 to find out how!

Make a "speedometer" for your spinning object.
- If you can see a single spot on a rotating object appear in exactly the same place every flash, then you know that the time between your flashes is directly related to how fast it's spinning.
- Calculate speed as Revolutions per Minute (RPM) from the flash delay (your `strobeDelay` variable). Even without a display on the Arduino, you can still send and receive data using the serial port to display on the IDE's serial monitor. See page 24 for the "ins and outs" on Serial communication.
- So, how many milliseconds are in a second? Seconds in a minute? If the thing that's moving goes back to the exact same position when the flash goes on, then your RPM = Flashes per minute.

Persistence of Vision: Old Fashioned Brain Tricks

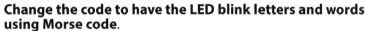

Things that move really quickly and change at the same time, show up as a single unchanging thing to our brains. The earliest example of this awesome effect is the thaumatrope: a paper disc with an image on both sides with string attached to the two outside edges. By twisting the string around, then pulling hard on either side of the string, the paper spins fast and it looks like the bird is in the cage! Try making your own and see what kind of crazy mixed up combinations you can make.

SmartBot's Thinking Lab: Stroboscope-on-a-rope!

A strobe (or stroboscope) is basically a light that turns on and off really fast. It can help you see things that spin or move faster than you could normally see. To make a strobe work for something, it has to be timed to turn on right when the thing you're looking at is in the same place it was last time.

When it's dark, each flash makes it look like the object being lit has stopped, or is moving really slowly. Our brains do a thing called *persistence of vision* that strings together all the pictures that come into our eyes into something that looks like our moving thing is just standing still, because the only images our eyes ever get are the ones with the moving thing in the exact same place. This effect can also works backwards, making still things look like they're moving (like a movie, cartoon, or zoetrope)!

In the code for this project, the number from our potentiometer (or that we entered by hand) is used to calculate how far apart the flashes are on the Arduino. When each flash matches up to the fan blade in a dark room, persistence of vision takes over, and it really seems like it's slowed down. To make the fan blade appear to stop completely, the fan speed and flash would have to match perfectly, and that's really, really hard to do. Why? Well, your fan is not a precision instrument that spins reliably at the same rate. So the "perfect" flash delay changes a little bit every time the fan spins around.

With really fast moving parts like fans or engine pistons, it's impossible to get a good look at what's going on while it's moving if you don't have your trusty stroboscope.

Harold "Doc" Edgerton was an amazing inventor, explorer, and MIT professor who pioneered the use of strobes in photography. His work allowed the creation of super-awesome high-speed photographs. "Doc" also invented some of the first cameras capable of capturing undersea life. A huge collection of Dr. Edgerton's amazing photos and videos are on the Web at *edgerton-digital-collections.org*

20 Reasons
Not To Stick Your Finger Into
a Moving Fan Blade

Remember folks, no matter how slow the fan looks using your strobe, it really is moving pretty fast, so just don't touch it.

1. Everyone will call you "stubby".
2. Fingers are your window to the world!
3. Fans move fast, your fingers probably don't, unless they're *Ninja fingers*.
4. They're called fan *blades* for a reason.
5. If you're so curious, turn the fan off, *then* touch it!
6. People *like* you, you're a *likable person*. People care that you have all your fingers.
7. Finger blood and electricity don't mix. Or at least, *they shouldn't*.
8. I heard of a crash test dummy who stuck his finger in a moving fan blade. Once the dust settled, all they found were his aluminum kneecaps, and grisly smile in a pile of rubble.
9. Just because it's moving doesn't make it cooler than when it's not. Just more chop-chop-choppy.
10. If you're already an adept master at juggling knives at high speeds, go for it! (just kidding)
11. High fives are much cooler than high *fours*.
12. Putting your finger in your nose might be safer.
13. Just think for a second... what other ***non-dangerous*** thing can you poke with your fingers?
14. You're smarter than that.
15. You may live, but you'll never live down being called, "That one kid who got maimed by a fan".
16. If you survive, your penmanship will probably not improve.
17. You'll only be able to point the finger of blame at yourself, If you even *have one* afterwards!!
18. If you still want to after all these reasons: Go for it, though you may not be at the top of your class, at least you'll have a great story to tell once your wounds heal into cool looking scars.
19. I told you not to, and I know better! *I wrote a book!*
20. Actually, yeah, never mind, it's a totally awesome idea to stick your finger in the moving fan blade, look it doesn't eve.. ***AUGH OH MY GLOB IT OW OW OW!! AAAAHHHHHH FIND MY FINGER!!!!***

PROJECT TWO

R.I.F.F.

For our second project, we'll be making what I call the "Randomly Influenced Finger Flute", or RIFF. With a little bit of code, you can make a kind of "musical instrument" that anyone can play! It doesn't take many parts to build, and it doesn't take an expert to play it. **_Let's go!_**

Parts Needed

- An Arduino. We like RedBoard and Uno.

- USB cable to upload to the Arduino.

- A speaker.

- A computer.

Have the Arduino software installed and ready. If you haven't done this yet, see page 4.

WHERE TO FIND PARTS

You can get Arduinos, jumper wires, LEDs, potentiometers and more at your local electronic component store, or online at great places like **SparkFun.com**, **Adafruit.com**, and **MakerShed.com**

Recycling:
You can get speakers from old talking toys or headphones if you are careful. *Note:* Only use speakers that have a paper or plastic diaphragm like the ones shown in this book. Don't use little buzzers or flat piezo speakers, they can damage your Arduino if used without a resistor.

Let's Build!

1. Plug your speaker wires into the Arduino.

Plug one speaker wire (it doesn't matter which one) into the GND (ground) pin. Then put the other speaker wire into one of the digital I/O pins. We're using pin 10, but you can use any pin you like, just as long as the code knows which one you chose.

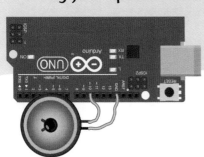

2. Input the code below into your IDE, verify it, and upload to the Arduino.

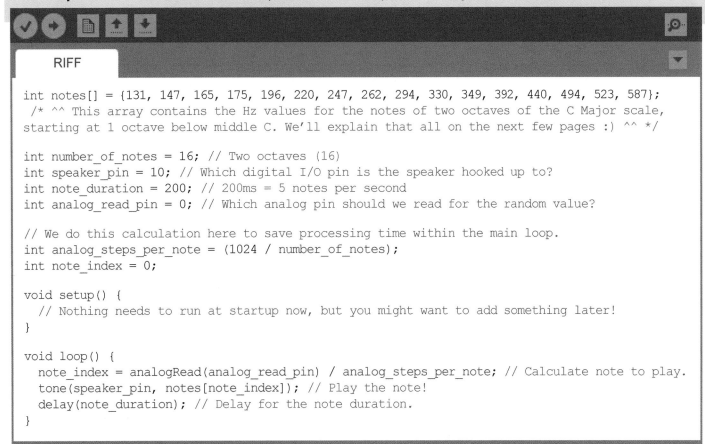

RIFF

```
int notes[] = {131, 147, 165, 175, 196, 220, 247, 262, 294, 330, 349, 392, 440, 494, 523, 587};
 /* ^^ This array contains the Hz values for the notes of two octaves of the C Major scale,
starting at 1 octave below middle C. We'll explain that all on the next few pages :) ^^ */

int number_of_notes = 16; // Two octaves (16)
int speaker_pin = 10; // Which digital I/O pin is the speaker hooked up to?
int note_duration = 200; // 200ms = 5 notes per second
int analog_read_pin = 0; // Which analog pin should we read for the random value?

// We do this calculation here to save processing time within the main loop.
int analog_steps_per_note = (1024 / number_of_notes);
int note_index = 0;

void setup() {
  // Nothing needs to run at startup now, but you might want to add something later!
}

void loop() {
  note_index = analogRead(analog_read_pin) / analog_steps_per_note; // Calculate note to play.
  tone(speaker_pin, notes[note_index]); // Play the note!
  delay(note_duration); // Delay for the note duration.
}
```

*More complete/updated code with named notes, and a lot more can be found at **superawesomebook.com/riff**, but why not test your typing skills and enter this into the Arduino program yourself? Comments are optional, but helpful!*

Innies and Outies

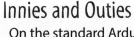

On the standard Arduino Uno, there are 14 general input/output pins, and 6 Analog input pins (which can also be configured to be outputs). Digital output pins can all be controlled to tell each one exactly when to turn on, and when to turn off. You can use them for lights, motors, or even talking to other computers! Digital input pins can tell if there's 5 volts going to them, or not (1 or 0). Analog input pins read voltage coming in on the wires plugged into them as a number between 0 and 1023, really useful for projects like the strobe where you need to carefully control something, or this project where you need lots of values in between fully on and fully off. Check out the Arduino diagram on **page 3** for a better idea of where stuff is located on the board.

EXPERIMENT TIME: R.I.F.F.

Gently touch the contacts under the analog pins of the Arduino with your finger and your Arduino will play you a tune. Our code takes the voltage wobble being read by the analog input pin and calculates a number to make a musical tone. The wobble makes it random — that's why it's called a "Randomly Influenced Finger Flute"!

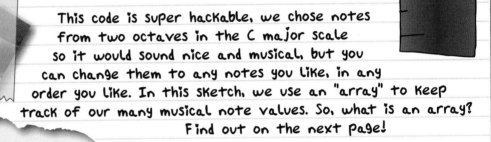

Keep one finger on Analog pin 0, and use your other fingers to touch pins like ground, 5v, or others to make lots of different sounds. As long as you're mostly free of static charge, it shouldn't hurt anything. Touching 5v usually results in higher tones, and touching ground gives you lower tones.

This code is super hackable, we chose notes from two octaves in the C major scale so it would sound nice and musical, but you can change them to any notes you like, in any order you like. In this sketch, we use an "array" to keep track of our many musical note values. So, what is an array? Find out on the next page!

Understanding Code

Debugging: What happens when your code doesn't work, but the compiler thinks it's fine? It's time to debug! Back when computers were the size of giant rooms, their components would get warm, and insects would make their way in and short-circuit the computer. We don't have to worry about that nowadays, but we still have to "debug" when our code isn't behaving. Luckily, we've got an easy method that can help.

Serial debugging: The serial port is a bit like a private text chat between the Arduino and the computer it's plugged into. You start the "chat" with a single line of code in the `setup()` function:

```
Serial.begin(9600);
```

Then in the main loop, you can make up a line of text or numbers to send out, like:

```
Serial.println("Something happened!");
```

To see this data, open the serial monitor in the IDE and you can see exactly what your Arduino program is telling you! You can also use the serial console window to send text commands *back* to your Arduino using the `Serial.read()` function (*See:* Examples > Communication > ReadASCIIString), but that's less for debugging, and more for controlling things!

24

Code Comments: Where am I? What are we doing?

Code can be hard to understand sometimes, so good coders leave little notes & hints about how something is supposed to be used, or how something is meant to work near the code they want to explain. This is super helpful, and you can write almost anything you want. Just put two slashes (//) before your comment, and everything after it will be gray and won't be code.

```
/* Multiple line comments use a slash and a star to start the
comment, and then a star and a slash to end the comment. */
```

What's an array?

So, we know a variable is like a happy little puppy we give a name, who will play fetch with us. When we have a whole bunch of numbers or other things to manage, we need an **array**. Add an empty set of square brackets after the name, and suddenly we have a bucket of puppies, otherwise known as an array!

Your dog variable is called by the same name, except with a number in square brackets at the end. The first one is 0, the second is 1, and on and on.

Let's say we want what the third puppy is holding. All we have to do is write `dog[2]` in our code and he'll give us a `'B'`. The best part is you can also put any `int` variable in place of the number in the brackets to pick which one you want. Just remember, all the dogs in the bucket have to be the same type, but you can have as many values as you want (within limits).

```
char dog[] = {'E','J','B'};
```

Analog in, Digital out, such pinteresting things!

On an Arduino, there are a whole bunch of little wire sockets, and most of them are connected to an actual "pin" on the Atmega computer chip on the Arduino. That's why we call them pins and not the sockets that they are, because we're thinking about them as being connected directly into the chip.

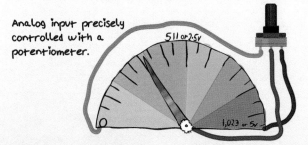

Analog input precisely controlled with a potentiometer.

"Untied" analog input randomly changed by electronic interference from the world.

So, how does the Arduino change the notes being played, without any other input? The answer is *noise!* Each of the analog inputs on the Arduino is a bit like this gauge. In the strobe project, we used a potentiometer to set the voltage to between 0 (Ground) and 5 volts. In this project, there is nothing attached to the analog input pins. Almost anything can push the electrical signal around when it's not "tied down". Without a strong signal, the value read by the Arduino wiggles and wobbles around from electronic noise! There's electricity everywhere you go, and without a wire attached, the charges build and disperse electricity everywhere, even from your body when you touch the pins.

25

Let's Play!
ScienceBot's Experiment Ideas

All science starts with a question. Here are a few to get your brain going.

What makes randomized music nicer to listen to? Is it the notes? How fast they're played?
- Don't forget: Science is about repeatability! Record different performances of your RIFF.
- Ask your friends which recording sounds best. If you play slower, does the music sound better? What if you reduce or expand the range of notes played by your RIFF? If you can read music, try changing your program so that the RIFF will only play the pitches in a simple children's folk song like "Twinkle Twinkle Little Star".
- If you ask enough people, you should be able to think about what makes a melody nice to listen to.

What range of sounds can you actually hear? Is it different than your friend? Or an adult?
- The numbers in the array are in Hertz (Hz). Sounds are measured in Hertz, which is a measure of the frequency of the sound vibrations per second.
- This requires changing the code to output more values. Just try some new numbers in the array! Some very large or small numbers you might not be able to hear, but you can probably feel with your fingers.
- Do some research on what humans should be able to hear, and see where *you* stand!

ear

BuilderBot's Challenges
These are some cool ideas to make your project look a little cooler, do more, or just get more organized.

Stick it in a mint tin (with insulation), including a battery and sound output headphone jack.
- Remember to insulate the bottom of the tin, or else you'll fry your poor Arduino! `~`
- If you're careful, you can make a notch in the side of the tin for your headphone jack plug, so when it closes it looks really snazzy.

Use a button and make it into a doorbell to play a random tune when someone arrives.
- You'll need to add a button and change the code to only turn on when the button is pushed, *See:* File > Examples > Digital > Button in the Arduino IDE.

Connect wires from the Analog, 5v, and ground pins to aluminum foil pads or thumb tacks to make it a lot easier to control.
- With a little practice you could even play it a bit like a piano.

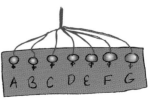

CoderBot's Challenges

Here are some more "advanced" challenges for coders who aren't afraid to look things up, try new things, be curious, and go nuts!

Add a button and a potentiometer to change the notes or style of play.

- You could add more arrays to store different sets of notes and select the different arrays based on some input. Or, since pitches are just number values, you could shift the values being played by adding or subtracting Hz based on a button or other analog input.
- *See:* Examples > Digital > Button

Add a distance sensor to make it play like an air piano.

- There are a bunch of small distance sensors that can plug straight into an Arduino, like an ultrasonic sensor, or an infrared sensor. They work by sending out light or sound, and measuring how late or how strong the return signal is.

- While reading from one, you can convert the distance it returns every half second into a note to play, almost like a Theremin!
- *See:* Examples > Sensors > Ping

Output the note signals as MIDI to control external instruments or trigger sounds from computers.

- Professional musical instruments have an awesome way to talk to each other called MIDI. It's a simple "chat room"-like connection that lets two devices have a conversation with each other in simple messages, like what note to play, and how loud.
- With just a little code, you can tell a MIDI piano or drum kit exactly what to play, based on any input you want, how cool is that?!
- *See:* Examples > Communication > MIDI

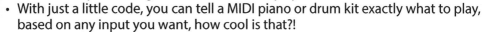

SmartBot's Thinking Lab: Random Music isn't Magic, it's Science!

So, how can something that makes an LED flash quickly *also* make a speaker work? Turns out, they work on the same principle. When the Arduino turns the digital output on and off really quickly, there's no middle. When you graph it, it looks like little squares on a line, this is called a **square wave**.

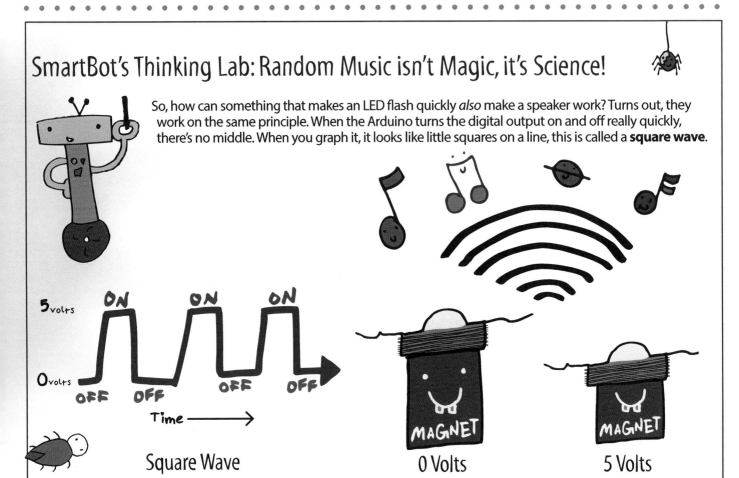

Square Wave

0 Volts

5 Volts

Hidden inside a standard speaker is a coil of copper wire, and a permanent magnet. When the Arduino sends 5 volts to the speaker's coil, it moves away/towards the magnet (depending on which wire you plugged into ground). When the voltage drops to 0, it springs back. 5 volts, move in/out — drop to 0, spring back. Again, and again! When you do this really quickly, you get *sound!* By using the `tone()` function on the Arduino, we send the speaker a **square wave** at a given rate, in hertz [**Hz**] (or number of on/off cycles per second). The higher the number, the higher the pitch.

In the RIFF code on the first line we make a bucket of variable puppies (an array of integers) called `notes`, and it's full of numbers. Each of these numbers, (unlike an *actual* bucket of actual puppies), is what the code picks from to send to the `tone()` function out to the speaker. These aren't just any old random numbers though, these are two *octaves* of the *C Major scale*, as measured in Hz.

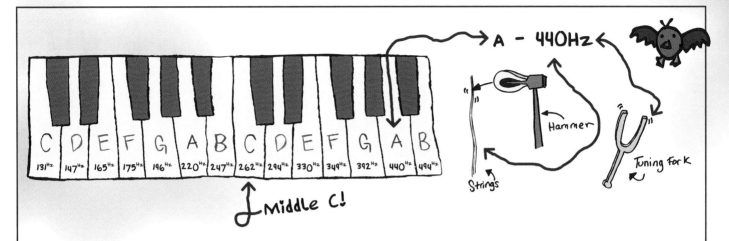

On a piano, the number of vibrations per second that the strings make when hit would be exactly the same as on your RIFF, starting on the C below middle, and going up from there. Though our RIFF program doesn't follow any real musical rules, it does stick to the notes we give it in the array. Using a musical note chart, we can program in almost any *musical scale.*

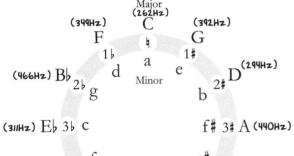

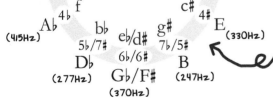

*Values rounded to the nearest whole Hertz for simplicity.

OCTAVE: is a grouping of 8 whole musical notes, labeled from A to G and then repeating the first letter again. When you repeat the starting letter, eight keys higher, it will vibrate exactly twice as fast.

SCALE: notes played in alphabetical order, and can begin on any letter between A and G. The musical scale of all white keys (on a piano) that starts on C is called "C Major".

This weird-looking thing is called the "Circle of Fifths". It describes how all musical "keys" (order of specific set of 8 notes) are related to each other, and can be used to figure out all sorts of interesting things about what is musical, and what tones are in harmony, and which are in dissonance (sound bad together). Picking notes that aren't in a major or minor key together might result in quite a sour tune!

PROJECT THREE

THE TAPPER!

For our last project, we will be building "The Tapper". Tap the speaker plugged into the Arduino, and then it plays a tune back to you on that same speaker. We'll learn how a regular speaker can be both an input, *and* an output in the same project! Afterwards, you can adjust this project to trigger almost anything you want.

Parts Needed

- An Arduino. We like RedBoard and Uno.

- USB cable to upload to the Arduino.

- One bright LED. Totally optional, but it makes everything look cooler.

- A speaker.

- A computer.

Have the Arduino software installed and ready. If you haven't done this yet, see page 4.

WHERE TO FIND PARTS

Did you skip ahead? Look back in previous sections for suggestions.

You can buy a kit with all the parts for all the projects in this book at **SparkFun.com/sylviakit**

Let's Build!

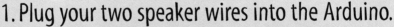

1. Plug your two speaker wires into the Arduino.

Plug one speaker wire (it doesn't matter which one) into the GND (ground) pin near the analog inputs. Then put the other speaker wire into analog pin 0. Which wire you connect to which pin will change how sensitive the tapper is. Both ways will work, so feel free to experiment. Plug an LED into pin 13 (long lead) and the short lead into any ground pin. You could just use the pin 13 light on the Arduino board, but the LED looks cooler.

2. Input the code below into your IDE, verify it, and upload to the Arduino."

Tapper

```
int ledPin = 13; // The pin we connect our LED to, if we have one.
int sensorPin = A0; // Analog pin we'll be reading from, connected to the speaker.
int tapTally = 0; // A placeholder for counting the number of taps.

void setup() {
  pinMode(ledPin, OUTPUT); // Use our ledPin as an output.
}

void loop() {
  // Did we sense a tap from the speaker?
  if (analogRead(sensorPin) > 50) {
    tapTally++; // Add one to tapTally variable
    digitalWrite(ledPin, HIGH); // Turn on the LED to show each tap.
    delay(250); // Wait for 1/4 of a second so the speaker can finish moving.
  } else {
    digitalWrite(ledPin, LOW); // Turn the LED off if we don't sense a tap.
  }

  // Use one "=" to set a value, but use two "==" to check a value!
  if (tapTally == 3) {
    digitalWrite(ledPin, HIGH); // Turn the LED On when we get 3 taps!
    pinMode(sensorPin, OUTPUT); // Switch the Analog input into an output.

    play(262); // Play a tune! Can you guess what song this might be?
    play(196);
    play(196);
    play(220);
    play(196);
    play(247);
    play(262);

    tapTally = 0; // Put tapTally back to 0 so we can run again.
    pinMode(sensorPin, INPUT);
  }
}

// Our own custom function, play a given tone for 1/4 of a second.
void play(int hz) {
  tone(sensorPin, hz);
  delay(250);
  noTone(sensorPin); // Turn off the tone to leave a gap between notes.
  delay(50);
}
```

*More complete/updated code can be found at **superawesomebook.com/tapper**, but why not test your typing skills and enter this into the Arduino program yourself? CompilerBot needs some entertainment!*

EXPERIMENT TIME: THE TAPPER

When it's ready, your Arduino is going to be checking in every loop to see if there's some small (but measurable) amount of electricity coming into analog pin O. If it goes above that small amount, we say that we got a "tap," and we can tally it in our tapTally variable doggie.

We have to wait a little bit of time before we check again (otherwise we'll see our input bounce around like crazy because the top of the speaker basically acts like a spring). After waiting, we check tapTally to see if it equals the right number of taps, then trigger something to happen. In our code we flip the analog input into an output, and play a simple song right back through the same speaker, though you can change out the code to do anything, even stuff like turn on home appliances with a power switch tail (an Arduino-switchable plug that lets you turn on things that plug into a wall!), or maybe a string of lights, or whatever you can imagine. There's tons of ideas and projects available online to help give you inspiration.

You could use it as a door alarm, or maybe a trigger for a Rube Goldberg machine? A musical drum tapper? A simple metronome? Go nuts!

Understanding Code: Arduino Arithmetic and Function Frenzy!

Computers are great at math. All you need to be able to do is write the equation in a way that CompilerBot understands, and your Arduino will solve it super fast!

Arduino Arithmetic: As you might have guessed, writing a math problem in a sketch is almost exactly like writing it for a human! There are only a few little differences that you're sure to pick up quickly:

Arduino arithmetic always starts with the answer. For example, if you want to double the value of a variable named "g", you just need to write an equation that is the same as the sentence, *"g should equal g times 2"*. In real code, that would be: "g = g * 2".

−	Subtract
+	Add
/	Divide
*	Multiply
=	Equals
%	Modulo‡

‡ A fancy term for the remainder left when you divide two numbers.

Here are a few rules to get started:

1. Arduino C will do arithmetic for you, no equals sign needed! For example, 5 is the same as 1+4 or 1+(2*2). Standard order of operations will be followed.

```
g = g * 1023 * 7;
```

2. Variables with a number type can be used in place of numbers.

```
int g = 6;
g = g * 2;
```
"g" now equals 12!

3. You can use the special shortcuts "++" and "--" to add 1 or subtract 1 from a variable.

```
g++; // g now equals 13
g--; // g now equals 12 again
```

Challenge time!

Can you figure out what the variable "**fang**" equals at the end of each of these examples? Each example assumes "**fang**" equals 3 at the start.

```
int fang = 3; // Define "fang" as an integer equal to 3
```
A. fang = fang + 4 + fang;   **C.** fang = 10 % fang;
B. fang = (42 / 6) * 2;   **D.** fang = 12 + (5 % 5)-(3 * (2+2));

Answers: A. 10, B. 14, C. 1 D. 0

Function Frenzy:
Usually when you write your first Arduino programs, you use a lot of functions created by other people. Did you know you can define your very own functions too? It's easy!

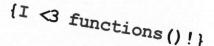

This simplified custom function from the Tapper code plays a sound for ¼ of a second. **Here's what's what:**

Return Data Type
The first word of a function says what kind of thing it returns when it's finished. This function just plays a sound, and doesn't make a number or something else, so we just say "**void**" here, because void means nothing!

Function Name
This is the function's name: "play". From now on, when we put the word in our code with parentheses after it: "**play()**", this "calls" the function, and the code inside the curly braces "{...}" runs!

```
void play (int hz) {
  tone(sensorPin, hz);
  delay(250);
}
```

Function Code
These sideways mustache curly braces hold our function code. Anything between these two will run when the function is called, and only when it's called. When the function is done, the program goes back to where it was and continues to run right after where the function was called.

Global Variable
Variables made at the *top* of a sketch are "global", they can be used anywhere! Variables made inside functions can *only* be used **in** that function.

Argument(s)
This is where you put in the "arguments" for a function, a list of variables separated by commas you want to give to your function code. So when the sketch gets to the line **play(262)**, it will call the function "play" with the 1st argument 262. The value for the variable **hz** is now **262** in the function code.

35

Let's Play!

ScienceBot's Experiment Ideas

All science starts with a question. Here are a few to get your brain going.

What are sound waves? How are they different from a physical knock or touch from your hand?

- Would a speaker work in space?
- Could a sound wave ever be stronger than your hand? (*Hint*: The MythBusters might know, but they call it a shock-wave!)

What's the lightest you can tap and still trigger it? How can you measure the size of your taps?

- The analog input on the Arduino is pretty sensitive and can help you figure this out, but remember you've got to watch out for electronic noise!

How fast does sound move through certain objects? Can putting down layers of paper or card stock interfere with the taps?

- Try to map the strength of your taps with the analog value over time, and you should see peaks and valleys. Notice it echoes or bounces. Why is that?

BuilderBot's Challenges

These are some cool ideas to make your project look a little cooler, do more, or just get more organized.

Tape a ruler to the speaker to trigger it with a knock or something lighter than a finger tap.

Hook the speaker up under a marble-drop in a Rube Goldberg machine to trigger the next step with a servo.

Add a logic level amplified microphone so when a person speaks, it interrupts with a tone!

CoderBot's Challenges

These are "advanced" challenges for coders who aren't afraid to look things up, try new things, be curious, and go nuts!

Make the tap trigger programmable… with taps!

- *Hint*: Count, save for later, then test.
- Have it trigger only when a properly timed sequence of taps happens. A secret knock!
- *Hint*: Timing is already there, start small and simple.

Tap a little song, and after a little while without taps, it'll play back the same pattern.

- *Hint*: Timing is everything.

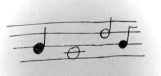

SmartBot's Thinking Lab: Electromagnetism

Sooo, how can a speaker that makes noise (as an output), tell our Arduino what's going on in the world (as an input)? It's **electromagnetism**!

Do you remember how the speaker moved when we gave it a little current with the Arduino tone function on the RIFF project? That electricity flowed into a coil of wire (a little loop) around an iron core. This is *all* you need to make an electromagnet! This electromagnetic force pushed the coil up or down, and is attached to a diaphragm made of plastic or paper, which pushes against the air and makes our sound. But did you know that this force also works *backwards?!*

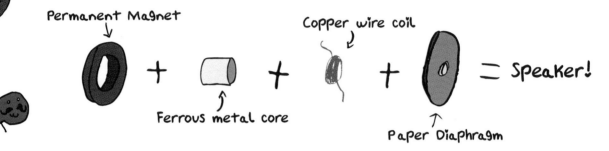

Permanent Magnet + Ferrous metal core + Copper wire coil + Paper Diaphragm = Speaker!

When you push or move the speaker coil through the magnetic field of its magnet, you also make a tiny current back through its wires! Speakers aren't really made for it, but in this way, they can be used as microphones! Everything you say can be picked up as teeny tiny currents from the speaker, and just the same, when you tap or move the diaphragm with your finger, it generates a larger amount of electricity that is much easier to detect with the Arduino on its analog input ports.

This same effect is used to turn a regular electric motor into a generator. By simply spinning an electric motor with something like a propeller, you can make your own electricity. Don't just sit around reading about it, go give it a try!

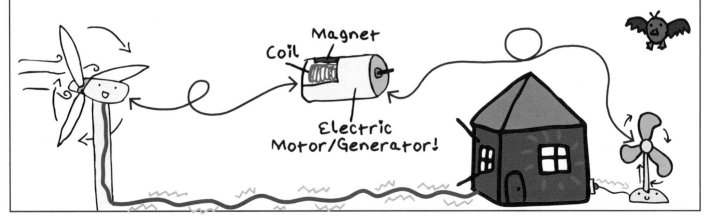

Coil Magnet

Electric Motor/Generator!

MAKE MORE!

SuperAwesomeBook.com

More Cool Arduino Projects, Resources, Links, and Videos

Looking for more details, code or even more crazy projects to do with your Arduino? I'm glad you asked! Check out our website for everything you need to help you with the projects found in this book, and resources and links to a bunch of others that we think you'll like.

Other Arduino Ideas

I bet you want some MORE ideas. Well, you're in luck! I love Arduino soooo much and there are so many ideas that I can think of. Here are five of them. Also, you can always look on the internet to find some other ideas too!

RGB LED strips! – You can use an Arduino to control individually addressable LED strips or Christmas lights! Program them to chase or make a game out of it and wrap it around your waist or hat or whatever. Perfect for any holiday.

Spy door alarm! – Take your Arduino, attach a distance sensor, and program it so when something moves in front of the sensor, your Arduino sends an alarm. You can use a buzzer, or maybe some type of LCD screen or just some LED's to start flashing and beeping!

Self driving car! – Add a GPS thingie to your Arduino and attach to an RC car. Program your car to drive itself from point A to point B.

Arduino go! – Make a game. Add an LCD screen to your Arduino with time and alarms on it. Include a piezo buzzer and GPS thingie so when an alarm goes off, you have to get to the place where you're going to turn it off!

Arduino bear! – Put an Arduino in a teddy bear to make it flash lights and use the Adafruit WAV shield to make him talk. You could even add
Bluetooth and control it all with your phone or the internet. Tweeting bear? :D

Places to Purchase Parts and Boards

Sylvia's Project Kit – Get a kit of all the parts you need for the projects in this book at – **sparkfun.com/sylviakit**
Sparkfun – Parts, kits, and resources including Arduino tutorials – **learn.sparkfun.com/tutorials/what-is-an-arduino**
Adafruit – Parts, kits, videos, and a series of guides to learn more about the Arduino – **learn.adafruit.com/category/learn-arduino**
MakerShed – Purchase Arduino boards and accessories – **makershed.com**

Online Arduino Resources

Arduino website – The home of the Arduino. Contains code, drivers, troubleshooting, and more – **www.arduino.cc**
Make Magazine Arduino – Videos, project ideas, how-tos, kits, parts, and blog posts about what people are doing around the world with the Arduino – **makezine.com/category/electronics/arduino/**
Instructables Arduino Projects – Offers a number of Arduino projects at varying levels of complexity – **instructables.com/id/Arduino-Projects/**
Lilypad Arduino – An Arduino board for projects using textiles and wearable electronics – **lilypadarduino.org**

Recommended Books

GET OUT THERE & MAKE SOMETHING!

Getting Started with Arduino – A handy little guide to getting started on Arduino by Massimo Banzi, the father of Arduino – **www.amzn.to/YoR8Rv**
Programming Arduino: Getting Started with Sketches - By Simon Monk. Clear, easy-to-follow downloadable examples show you how to program Arduino in C. This is a must have book for learning to use the Arduino – **www.amzn.to/YWlrCE**

I hope you enjoyed this book as much as I loved making it!
'Till the next book, GET OUT THERE AND MAKE SOMETHING!!!!! :D

ARTBOT'S DOODLE CORNER!